Ancient
World

Communication
in the Ancient World

Crabtree Publishing Company
www.crabtreebooks.com

Life in the Ancient World

Contributing authors: Paul Challen, Shipa Mehta-Jones,
  Lynn Peppas, Hazel Richardson
Publishing plan research and development:
  Sean Charlebois, Reagan Miller
  Crabtree Publishing Company
Editors: Kathy Middleton, Adrianna Morganelli
Proofreaders: Kathy Middleton, Marissa Furry
Editorial director: Kathy Middleton
Photo research: Katherine Berti, Crystal Sikkens
Designer and prepress technician: Katherine Berti
Print and production coordinator: Katherine Berti

Cover description: (Front right) Scribes in ancient Egypt are often depicted sitting with crossed legs and a scroll in their lap. Examples of ancient writing include Norse runes (front left), Egyptian heiroglyphs (back top), Mesopotamian cuneiform (front middle), Mayan glyphs (front top), and Greek inscription (back bottom).

Title page description: Centuries ago, battle commands were carried by horse and rider from leader to leader.

Illustrations:
William Band: pages 13, 18 (bottom), 23 (right), 30 (right)
Antoinette "Cookie" Bortolon: page 21
James Burmester: page 9 (left)
Crabtree Publishing Company: page 21 (bottom)
Lauren Fast: page 24
Roman Goforth: page 7 (bottom)
Rosie Gowsell: page 16 (middle)
Ole Skedsmo: page 10 (left)

Photographs and reproductions:
Alamy: © The Art Archive: page 26 (left); © Manor Photography:
  page 28
Bridgeman Art Library: page 25 (top)
Corel: title page
Dreamstime: page 20 (left)
Fotosearch: pages 6
iStockphoto.com: pages 14, 19 (top)
Wikimedia Commons: page 12 (right); Nihonshoki Tanaka:
  page 4 (top); Gavin Collins: page 4 (left), 8; zayzayem: page 9;
  Sailko: page 11 (right); Marie-Lan Nguyen: page 11 (middle
  and top); Rama: cover; page 17 (top); Hans Hillewaert:
  page 17 (bottom); Piero d'Houin dit Triboulet: page 18 (top);
  Rosemania: page 20 (right); Claus Ableiter: page 23; Association
  of Cultural Properties: page 27; kyz: page 29 (bottom); I. Berig:
  page 30 (bottom); Icelandic National Library: page 31
J.M. Kenoyer, Courtesy Sept. of Archaeology and Museums Govt.
  of Pakistan: page 12 (bottom left)
Courtesy Japan Studies Institute: page 26 (top)
Photos.com: page 15
All other images by Shutterstock.com

Library and Archives Canada Cataloguing in Publication

CIP available at Library and Archives Canada

Library of Congress Cataloging-in-Publication Data

Communication in the ancient world.
   p. cm. -- (Life in the ancient world)
  Includes index.
  ISBN 978-0-7787-1733-1 (reinforced library binding : alk. paper) -- ISBN 978-0-7787-1740-9 (pbk. : alk. paper) -- ISBN 978-1-4271-8799-4 (electronic pdf) -- ISBN 978-1-4271-9640-8 (electronic html)
  1. Communication--History--To 1500--Juvenile literature. I. Crabtree Publishing Company. II. Title.

  P91.2.C86 2011
  302.2--dc23

                                                2011029191

Crabtree Publishing Company

www.crabtreebooks.com   1-800-387-7650

Printed in Canada/082011/MA20110714

Published in Canada
Crabtree Publishing
616 Welland Ave.
St. Catharines, Ontario
L2M 5V6

Published in the United States
Crabtree Publishing
PMB 59051
350 Fifth Avenue, 59th Floor
New York, New York 10118

Published in the United Kingdom
Crabtree Publishing
Maritime House
Basin Road North, Hove
BN41 1WR

Published in Australia
Crabtree Publishing
3 Charles Street
Coburg North
VIC, 3058

Contents

Communication in the Ancient World

Most historians agree that a civilization is a group of people that shares common languages, some form of writing, advanced technology and science, and systems of government and religion. Without the creation of a form of written communication, ancient civilizations could not have thrived.

Reading, Writing, and Record-keeping

With written communication, the privileged became educated and learned to read and write. Record-keeping also became important to every ancient civilization. Each civilization's history of battles, myths, and legends, which had previously been passed from one generation to the next through memorization and story-telling, was recorded and saved for future generations to read. Business transactions, hymns, marriages, and legal proceedings were also recorded. Eventually, through trade and travelers, written language introduced new methods of farming, different religions, and education to other civilizations.

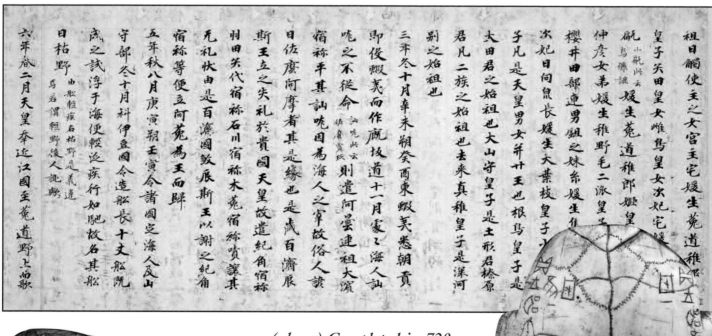

(above) Completed in 720 A.D., the Nihon Shoki, *also known as* The Chronicles of Japan, *is the second-oldest book in Japanese history. The book begins with the creation myth, and ends with accounts of events in the 8th century.*

(left) Halley's Comet is visible from Earth every 75 years. This clay tablet has a record of the comet being observed in 164 B.C. in Babylon, Iraq.

Shang priests, in China, put questions on oracle bones and then looked for answers in the cracks made when the bones were heated.

Maps and Timeline of Ancient Civilizations

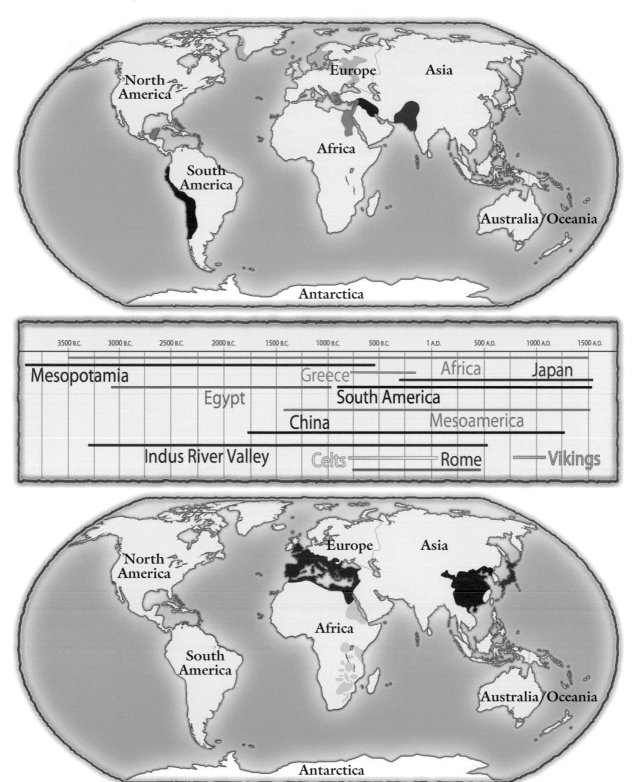

The period described as ancient history is usually defined as the time from first recorded history up to the Early Middle Ages, around 300 A.D. Some of the civilizations in this book begin well after the ancient period but are included because they were dominant early civilizations in their regions. The beginning and ending dates of early civilizations are often subject to debate. For the purposes of this book, the timelines begin with the first significant culture in a civilization and end with the change or disappearance of the civilization. The end was sometimes marked by an event such as invasion by another civilization, or simply by the gradual dispersion of people due to natural phenomena such as famine or earthquakes.

Ancient China

The ancient Chinese developed their own language and systems of writing and record-keeping. A standard written language became a necessity when the warring states in China first became unified in 221 B.C. It meant the emperor's commands could be understood by everyone across the vast country. Technical advances, such as the development of inks and paper, allowed the ancient Chinese to record history, keep track of time, and add and subtract numbers.

Spoken Language

Over hundreds of years, the spoken Chinese language went through several changes. During the Zhou dynasty, Old, or Archaic, Chinese was spoken. Not much is known about what Old Chinese sounded like. During the time of the Sui, Tang, and Song dynasties, a new form of the Chinese language, known as Middle Chinese, was used. By 1000 A.D., a number of different dialects, or versions, had emerged, many of which survive today.

Writing Systems

Writing was first used in China for religious ceremonies. In 1400 B.C., Shang religious leaders, or priests, carved questions to the gods on sheep bones and turtle shells. These bones became known as oracle bones. By about 400 B.C., artisans began writing on bamboo strips, wooden tablets, and coated silk cloth using ink made from soot or charcoal mixed with water and glue. Writing usually described great historical events, such as military battles or the rise of an emperor. Government officials during the Qin dynasty introduced a standardized form of writing across China to ensure that educated people understood the emperor's commands.

Before paper was available, bamboo was used to write on. Chinese characters were cut into thin strips of bamboo beginning at the top.

Writing Without An Alphabet

China does not have an alphabet that combines letters to form words like other languages. Chinese writing uses characters, or symbols, to represent words and ideas. There are about 40,000 Chinese characters and each one can be made up of as many as 26 brushstrokes. To read a Chinese newspaper, a person might need to know about 3,000 of these characters. Most Chinese characters have changed very little since the Qin dynasty, when the emperor ordered that writing be standardized.

Date		
1700 B.C.–1400 B.C.	𜸀	𜸁
776 B.C.–250 B.C.	𜸂	𜸃
250 B.C.–25 A.D.	𜸄	𜸅
25 A.D.–200 A.D.	漁	馬
380 A.D.–Present	漁	馬

Ancient Calculators

The ancient Chinese called mathematics *suan chu,* or "the art of calculation." Number symbols found on oracle bones from the Shang dynasty date back 3,400 years. Chinese numbers are based on the decimal system, or the number ten, just as most number systems are today. The ancient Chinese used mathematics for many purposes, such as building construction, flood control, and to calculate sums for trading goods.

The Chinese Calendar

Mathematics was used to develop the Chinese calendar. The ancient Chinese divided each year into twelve months. Unlike other calendars that are based on the cycles of the sun, the Chinese calendar is based on the cycles of the moon. One full lunar phase of 28 days represents a month. The cycles of the moon are different from the cycles of the sun, so Chinese New Year happens each year between late January and early February instead of on January 1.

The Chinese Zodiac

The ancient Chinese developed a system for keeping track of the years using twelve different animals. According to a legend, the zodiac originated with **Buddhism**. The **Buddha** called all the animals of China to his bedside but only twelve came. To honor the animals for coming, he created a year for each one. Each animal has its own characteristics. Some Chinese believe that people born in a certain year will have the characteristics of that year's animal. A person born in the year 1995 was born in the Chinese Year of the Pig, and would be caring and determined.

1 2 3 4 5 6 7 8 9

The signs used for the numbers one through nine during the Shang dynasty are shown on the left.

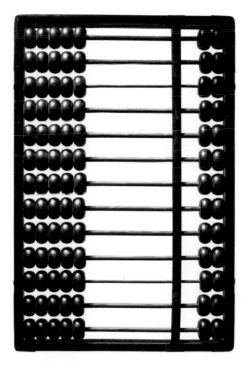

The Chinese invented the abacus, a counting tool that used rods and sliding beads. The abacus is still used in some parts of China.

Public Education

Education became very important during the Han dynasty. Around 100 B.C., Emperor Wudi agreed with the great Chinese thinker Confucius, that the key to good government depended on education. Wudi started a system of public schools for boys in every part of China that taught the ideas of Confucius. In the capital of China, there was a major school called the Grand School. The Grand School started out with only 50 students but within 100 years it had more than 30,000 students!

Ancient Mesopotamia

3900 B.C.–539 B.C.

The remains of ancient Mesopotamia lie between the banks of the Tigris and Euphrates rivers, in modern-day Iraq. Writing first began here as a system of record-keeping for administrators and traders. In about 3500 B.C., pictographs, or shapes that represent whole words or groups of words, were etched onto clay tags and attached to bags of grain so farmers could keep track of how much grain they had. Over time, the use of pictographs changed into a written language. This writing system is called cuneiform. Cuneiform is one of the oldest known writing systems.

Writing

Cuneiform was a form of writing in which words or ideas were represented by characters made up of triangles and straight lines. The characters were pressed into wet clay tablets using a reed **stylus**. The characters represented groups of sounds, syllables, or entire words that often meant different things depending on how they were used. Cuneiform was invented by the Sumerians, but it was adopted by the Akkadians, Hittites, Assyrians, and Babylonians, all of whom made their homes in the region called Mesopotamia.

The Talk of the Town

Mesopotamia was home to many different groups of people, each with their own spoken language. The language spoken by the Sumerians is not spoken today. The Akkadians were the first Mesopotamians to speak a Semitic language, or a language belonging to a group of related languages that also includes Hebrew and Arabic. The Akkadian language changed over time. Forms of the language were used by the Assyrians and the Babylonians. Each of these groups adapted cuneiform script slightly to its own languages.

This shows an account of silver written in Sumerian cuneiform on a clay tablet.

Writing on the Wall

Cuneiform changed when scribes realized that characters could represent sounds as well as objects. Scribes started using characters that represented small words as syllables, or parts, of larger words. By stringing together three short words, the scribes could create the sound of a long word. The association between characters and sounds meant that far fewer characters were required, because there were far fewer sounds than there were objects. The rebus, a type of modern-day puzzle, also uses the sounds of words to represent syllables.

Poetry

Poetry was an important form of spoken and written literature. The first Mesopotamian poet known by name was Enheduanna. She was a **priestess** and the daughter of a king. In one of Enheduanna's poems, the goddess Inanna is a ferocious warrior. In another, the poet writes about Inanna's role in ruling over civilization, as well as home and children.

The Library of Nineveh

The Assyrian king, Ashurbanipal, ordered his **scribes** to copy and collect cuneiform clay tablets from across the region to keep in the capital, Nineveh. This formed the first library of Mesopotamia, containing over 22,000 works, including some copies of earlier Sumerian and Akkadian texts. Ashurbanipal's collection included works on science, medicine, astronomy, religion, and folk tales. Modern researchers studying Mesopotamia use the vast Library of Nineveh as their primary source for many ancient texts.

Passing Time

The priests of Mesopotamia studied the position of the stars, the planets, the moon, and the sun, and they used this information to calculate dates and the start of seasons. The original Sumerian day was broken into 12 hours, with six hours of daylight and six hours of darkness. The new day began at sunset. The length of an hour changed to match the amount of daylight at different times of the year. The twelve-month calendar also originated in Sumer. Sumerian months were lunar, or based on the movements of the moon. Each month began with the full moon. The Babylonians later introduced the seven-day week.

Numbering Systems

Mesopotamians based their counting system on the number 60. Sixty can be divided in half (30), thirds (20), quarters (15), fifths (12), sixths (10), and tenths (6). The Assyrians used the base-60 system to become the first people to divide a circle into 360 degrees. The Mesopotamians were among the first people to use the number zero, and to use a number system for weights and measurements.

𒁹 1   𒌋 10

𒁹 60   𒐕 600

Mesopotamians etched symbols, which represented numbers, into cuneiform clay tablets.

Epic of Gilgamesh

The Epic of Gilgamesh tells the myth of Sumerian King Gilgamesh of Uruk. The stories in the epic teach lessons about the meaning of friendship, fears of sickness and death, and the search for everlasting life. Over time, these stories were collected into one long poem that was passed from one Mesopotamian civilization to another. Later civilizations added more tales and wrote new versions of others.

In the story, Gilgamesh (below) and his friend Enkidu cut off the head of the demon Humbaba, guardian of the cedar forests of Lebanon.

Scribe's School Life

Schools in Mesopotamia were called *e-dubbas*, meaning "Tablet House." Only boys were allowed to attend. The schools, developed by priests, began training young boys as scribes to read and write cuneiform. Students attended from sunrise to sunset, beginning in early youth and continuing into their young adulthood. They only had about six days off from school every month—three holy days and three free days. Young scribes who spoke without permission or were late for school were punished with lashes from a stick or cane.

All in a Day's Work

The first thing a young boy learned in school was how to make a clay tablet and how to hold a reed stylus properly. He memorized long lists of cuneiform symbols and the meanings of each symbol. Young scribes also learned the history of Mesopotamia, both from clay tablets that retold the events of the kings' reigns and from poetry. Scribes studied math and astrology so they could make calendars, and they learned law codes. Scribes learned to diagnose illnesses and to create medicine. To prepare them for life in the priesthood, young boys were taught divining, the art of reading the will of the gods, and of predicting the future.

A scribe learn to write copied cuneiform on a wet clay tablet. If he made a mistake, the clay was smoothed over and the scribe tried again.

The Record Keepers

Once they were fully trained, scribes had an essential role in society as the recorders of facts, figures, ideas, and traditions. Many scribes worked as secretaries, book-keepers, accountants, archivists, recorders, and writers of **hymns** and epics. Some scribes sat at city gates and hired out their writing services to **illiterate** clients. In some parts of modern-day Iraq and other Middle Eastern countries, this service still exists. Other scribes in ancient Mesopotamia became doctors and diviners.

A scribe during Sumerian times was an important man because of his ability to write. Scribes were hired by people who could not read and write to write letters and record business transactions.

Cylinder Seals

Mesopotamians often employed scribes to write important business documents for them on tablets of soft clay. The tablets were then "signed" by the sender by rolling a personalized cylinder seal across it. The seal was similar to a signature, and only used by the owner. Cylinder seals were used on ancient documents for about 3,000 years. The seals were rarely more than two inches (five centimeters) high. They were most often made of stone but were sometimes made of bone, ivory, glass, metal, wood, or sun-dried or baked clay. They were carved with miniature animals, gods, and other figures, as well as cuneiform characters. Very skilled craftspeople carved the design backwards, so that it would come out the right way when rolled across the clay.

Mesopotamian cylinder seals were often made from a hard stone such as limestone. The seals were then rolled in wet clay to form an impression.

seal   *impression*

seal   *impression*

Written in Stone

The best known Mesopotamian collection of laws was the Code of King Hammurabi. This ancient code was carved into eight-foot (three-meter) tall stones that were placed around the kingdom for all to see. The laws were very strict, stating the rule of "an eye for an eye, a tooth for a tooth." The 282 laws of Hammurabi's code dealt with family, labor, trade, and property.

(right) Hammurabi receives the code of laws from Shamash, the god of Justice.

Ancient Indus River Valley

Two of the world's greatest ancient civilizations began in the Indus River Valley, in what is now Pakistan—the Harrapans and the Aryans. The Harappans developed a system of writing which they used to record events and trade they did with other peoples. The Aryans' Sanskrit language is still used today in religious ceremonies.

3300 B.C.–550 A.D.

Harappan Symbols

Harappan writing has been found on many pieces of pottery and stone. Some of it dates from 3500 B.C., which means that the Harappans were one of the first civilizations to use writing. Like other ancient civilizations, such as the Egyptians, early Harappan writing was based on pictographs which made up a type of alphabet.

Harappan writing is a mystery to people today. No more than 20 symbols were ever carved on a tablet or seal. Nobody knows why or has been able to decipher the script. Researchers think that each symbol stands for a syllable rather than a letter and that the language was similar to Dravidian, a language still spoken by peoples in southern India.

An Ancient Tongue

The Aryans brought two languages with them when they came to the Indus Valley in about 1500 B.C.—Dardic, which has since disappeared, and Sanskrit.

Sanskrit is called an Indo-European language because it developed in the area between Europe, India, and Asia. It is similar to Latin, used in ancient Rome and ancient Greek. The Sanskrit word for mother is "matr," and the word for father is "pitr." In Latin, these words are "mater" and "pater." Today, Sanskrit is used only by brahmans, the Hindu priests, to read and write religious books, but some Sanskrit words are found in many modern languages, including Thai.

Written Sanskrit

The ancient Indians did not develop a written system of Sanskrit for more than 1,000 years. Their holy books, the Vedas, were memorized and passed down from brahman to brahman. The first known Sanskrit writing is a copy of the Rig Veda holy book written around 400 B.C.

An Ancient Unicorn

All Harappan trade goods had a pottery seal attached to them. Seals had writing and an image of an animal on them. Sometimes the animal was an elephant, a rhinoceros, or a bull, which represented gods. A unicorn was the most common image on seals. Some historians think that the unicorn was the symbol of the Harappan people or government. Around 1900 B.C., when the Harappan civilization started to decline, the unicorn image was no longer made on seals.

(left) The Harappans had about 300 symbols which were simplified to make carving easier. Symbols ran from left to right on the top line, and then from right to left on the next.

(above) Harappan seals had a carved inscription on top of a depiction of a scene or animal.

The Reign of Asoka

Asoka was one of India's most famous rulers. In 260 B.C., Asoka made Buddhism the official religion of his kingdom. Asoka ordered thousands of stone pillars and stupas, or monuments whose domed shape is said to represent the Buddha, to be raised across India. The stupas were carved to show laws on how to behave. These laws were known as dharma.

Buddhism was spread throughout India and the rest of Asia by traveling **monks** and holy men. Many people adopted the religion because they felt it helped relieve their suffering. The Buddha's teachings developed into a religion that still exists today, 2,500 years after the Buddha was born.

Hindu Literature

The ancient Indians wrote the world's longest story. It is called the *Mahabharata*, and was written in about 200 A.D. The most famous part of it is called the *Bhagavad-Gita*, or Song of the Lord. It is a very long poem about a warrior who talks to a god called Lord Krishna, who is disguised as a chariot driver.

India's greatest poet and playwright, Kalidasa, lived sometime between 450 A.D. and the early 500s A.D. Little is known about his life. A follower of the goddess Kali, Kalidasa is said to have prayed to the goddess, who rewarded him with his great gift for words. Kalidasa wrote long poems in Sanskrit. The plays he wrote, all of which have happy endings, were the first known plays performed in India.

Rama and Hanuman

One famous piece of Indian literature is the *Ramayana*, written in 200 A.D. It is the story of Prince Rama, who is sent to a forest for fourteen years by a rival half-brother and his jealous mother. While Rama is away, his wife, Sita, is kidnapped by a wicked demon. Rama finds her with the help of his friend, Hanuman, the monkey.

Sacred Books

The Vedas are a collection of hymns, stories, and rituals of the ancient Indians. They are a record of what life was like 4,000 years ago in India. The four Veda books, the *Rig Veda*, *Sama Veda*, *Yajur Veda*, and the *Atharva Veda* are studied by religious scholars, historians and linguists, or people who study and compare languages. There are many other ancient Indian books. The *Mahabharata* and the *Ramayana* are thought to be the longest poems in any language and each take up several books. The *Mahabharata* is the legend of a group of Aryans called the Bharatas. The *Ramayana* is a love poem.

An ancient scholar works on a Veda, or holy book, written in Sanskrit.

Ancient Greece

800 B.C.–146 B.C.

The ancient Greeks left the world an amazing legacy of art, architecture, and literature. They developed their own language and system of numbers, and became the founders of mathematics, science, and philosophy. They also created myths, or stories about the lives of the gods, goddesses, and heroes they believed ruled life on Earth.

A Universal Language

By about 1500 B.C., Greek-speaking people were established in Greece, probably having come as **invaders** from the north. There were a number of dialects of the Greek language, the most important of which were Attic, Doric, and Ionic. Ancient Greek was spoken on the Greek mainland, the Greek islands, Asia Minor, Italy, and Sicily. The political and cultural power of Athens made the Athenian dialect, Attic, the most spoken. From the Attic dialect there developed a version called *koine* which means "common" or "common to all the people." *Koine* became the standard form of ancient Greek. When the Greeks began conquering other people and colonizing other lands, *koine* became a common language. *Koine* was an important language in the Mediterranean and parts of Asia Minor and Africa for many centuries.

Pythagoras was a Greek scholar who started a school for boys and girls to study music, astronomy, and arithmetic. His methods of doing math are still used today.

Greece is the Word

The English word "alphabet" comes from the first two letters in the Greek alphabet, "alpha" and "beta." In 700 B.C., the Greeks adapted their alphabet from their neighbors, the Phoenicians. By 500 B.C., the Greeks made the Phoenician alphabet their own by adding five vowels and writing from left to right, as we do, and not right to left, as the Phoenicians did. The Greek alphabet has changed little since ancient times.

GREEK WORDS (English Translation)	ANCIENT GREEK MEANING	ENGLISH WORD
ΑΚΑΔΗΜΙΑ (akademeia)	The Academy	Academy
ΔΥΝΑΜΙΚΟΣ (dynamikos)	Powerful	Dynamic
ΠΟΙΗΤΗΣ (poietes)	Creator, poet	Poet
ΣΧΟΛΗ (schole)	Free time, leisure, discussion	School

School Days

Education was for the sons of wealthy Athenian families only. Boys started school at age seven and were taught to read and write, recite poetry from memory, and to play a musical instrument such as the lyre or flute. Education also included wrestling, boxing, running, and throwing a javelin and discus. Sports encouraged the competitive spirit and prepared young men to enter one of Greece's most popular sporting events, the Olympics. Girls in Athens did not go to school. They stayed home and learned spinning and weaving from their mothers. Some wealthy families hired private tutors who taught girls to read and write. In Sparta, girls trained to be strong so they could give birth to healthy babies who would grow up to be great soldiers.

Great Thinkers

The ancient Greeks were interested in learning the truth about human behavior. Thinkers known as philosophers studied why people act the way they do. The best known Greek philosophers were Socrates, Plato, and Aristotle. Socrates was interested in ethics, or the nature of right and wrong. He taught students to question everything to get at the truth. Aristotle was a tutor of Alexander the Great, who later conquered most of the world. Some Greek philosophers were scientists who studied plants and animals. In 335 B.C., Socrates' student, Plato, founded a school and library called the Academy, outside Athens. Plato believed that many things that could not be seen, such as human goodness, existed in the world.

Mythic Stories

Ancient Greeks explained disease, the weather, and earthquakes, by creating myths about gods that had the power to affect life on Earth. These myths, or stories, described the origin of the Earth, as well as the origins of the gods.

The Greeks also told stories about special human beings, descended from the gods, called heroes. The stories of these heroes, which often made points about human weaknesses and strength, were told by ancient Greek poets in long poems called epics. Epic poems were **oral** at first and written down many years later. The most famous Greek epics, the *Iliad* and the *Odyssey* were composed by a blind poet named Homer around 700 B.C.

Alexander the Great

By 338 B.C., Athens, Sparta, and most other Greek **city-states** were conquered by the king of Macedon. At age 20, his son Alexander, who would become known as Alexander the Great, conquered Egypt, India, and Persia. He thought highly of Greek culture and settled Greeks in the conquered cities. This preserved and spread Greek culture, as Alexander introduced Greek philosophy, language, art, and science to the captured cities. This period in history is known as the Hellenistic Age.

*Wealthy boys from Athens were taken to their lessons by a slave called a **paidogogus** (seen here sitting behind the pupil).*

Ancient Egypt

Over time, and until its defeat by the Roman Empire in 30 B.C., Egypt became one of the oldest and greatest of the ancient cultures. The ancient Egyptians were among the first to develop a written language. They borrowed a system from people who lived in Mesopotamia, in modern-day Iraq, and adapted it for their own use.

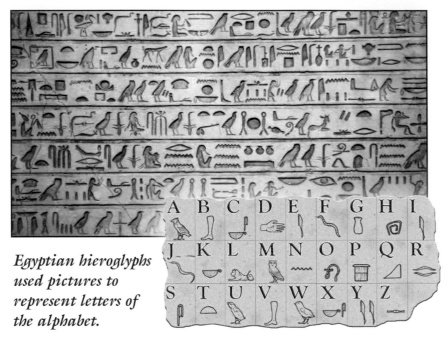

Egyptian hieroglyphs used pictures to represent letters of the alphabet.

Hieroglyphs

The Egyptians believed their written language was a gift from Thoth, god of wisdom. They thought writing was a holy process. The writing was later called hieroglyphs, or "sacred carvings," because they were often carved in stone on temple walls. A shortened version of hieroglyphs, called hieratic script, was used by priests.

The Egyptians used a writing system of more than 700 symbols, each representing an entire word, a syllable, or a letter of the alphabet. There were no vowels or punctuation. Often, hieroglyph "words" combined two symbols with sounds that people already knew to make one word. For example, to express the name of King Narmer, Egyptians drew a symbol of a fish, "nar" over a chisel, "mer."

Education

Only boys from wealthy or noble families attended school. They learned how to write with ink on papyrus and by carving hieroglyphs into pieces of clay. Older boys studied history, geography, science, and mathematics. Other boys learned a trade or craft from their fathers. Girls did not attend school, but girls from wealthy families were taught to read and write, and helped manage the estate. Some even trained at home to become doctors.

This column features an image of an ancient Egyptian noble and hieroglyphs that tell a story.

This statue of a scribe was carved around 2400 B.C. When writing, scribes sat cross-legged and used their kilts, or skirts, as surfaces to write on.

The Calendar

Farming calendars plotted the rise and fall of the Nile River's water, dividing the seasons according to its ebb and flow. In many ways, their division of the calendar year into three seasons is very similar to our own. As early as 3000 B.C., Egyptians had worked out a calendar of 365 days. It was based on the sun and had 12 thirty-day months plus five additional days. They invented this calendar by noting that the brightest star, Sirius, rose once a year, a moment or two before dawn. This seemed to predict the annual flood of the Nile and the ancient Egyptians fixed this event as the beginning of their calendar year.

The Scribe

Very few people could read in ancient Egypt. Young men, usually from noble families, were taught to write on papyrus and carve symbols into stone. These men were called scribes. Scribes recorded great battles, business transactions, temple records and prayers, stories, and songs. Some scribes wrote letters for people who could not read or write.

Alexander the Great

Alexander the Great invaded Egypt in 332 B.C. He made Greek the official language of Egypt. Greek soldiers, government workers, and businessmen arrived in Egypt and took the most important jobs. During Greek rule, the Egyptian religion was honored and temples continued to be built for their gods.

Written on stone

When Europeans explored Egypt in the 1700s, no one, including Egyptians of that time, could translate the writing and carvings. In 1798, while the French general Napoleon was fighting the British in Egypt, his soldiers discovered a black stone slab with three versions of the same message written on it. This slab was called the Rosetta Stone. It was the key that unlocked the mystery of a lost language. In 1822, a French scholar translated Egyptian hieroglyphs using inscriptions on the Rosetta Stone. The Rosetta Stone contains Greek, the everyday writing of ancient Egypt, called demotic, and hieroglyphs.

Ancient Africa

Birthplace of the earliest humans, Africa has been home to some of the world's oldest and most powerful civilizations, including the Egyptians, Nubians, the Aksumites, the Shona, and the Songhai. Each of ancient Africa's thousands of cultures developed its own spoken language or dialect, and some had written scripts. A number of universities in the ancient world were located in Africa. Many students came from afar to study at them.

Arabic Script

The most widely used script in ancient Africa was Arabic, the writing of the people who lived in what is now Saudi Arabia. Arabic spread through northern Africa and was adopted by the Sahel civilizations as they converted to **Islam**. At first, people spoke both their native language and Arabic. Eventually, Arabic script was used to write native languages.

Nubian Scripts

The Nubians in the kingdom of Kush developed a written language around 800 B.C. At first, they used Egyptian hieroglyphs to record their history and trade. After the Nubians moved their capital to Meroë, around 300 B.C., they developed their own written language. This was based on the ancient Egyptian script and had two forms: hieroglyphs and cursive. Hieroglyphs were inscribed on monuments. Cursive writing was simpler and was used for writing on papyrus. Archaeologists have decoded the sounds that the alphabet's symbols stood for, but they have not been able to translate the writing.

Ancient Nubian hieroglyphs were found on this tablet in the Nubian city of Meroë.

Aksumite Scripts

The Aksumites had three main scripts, or forms of writing: Arabic, Greek, and Ge'ez. Ge'ez was a language created by the Aksumites, and was similar to Arabic. Ge'ez script developed around 300 A.D. At first, there were only symbols for consonants, but the script was soon changed so that each symbol showed a syllable of a consonant and a vowel. There were 33 letters in Ge'ez, which were written from left to right.

Bantu Speakers

As the Bantu-speaking peoples, the Shona, migrated from western Africa, their languages combined with that of the other African peoples to create new languages. All ancient Bantu languages were spoken. In the 1700s, a written form of the language was developed. Today there are over 500 Bantu languages, spoken by 200 million people. The most common ones are Swahili, spoken on Africa's east coast, and Shona, spoken in Zimbabwe.

The symbols from the Aksumite language of Ge'ez were very similar to the Greek alphabet.

Watching, Listening, and Learning

Most ancient African children learned by watching adults carry out their work, by playing games, and by listening to stories. Children in all societies played a game called *mancala* to learn counting and mathematical skills. Children also learned by participating in initiation rituals, or knowledge ceremonies, in which they were taught about such things as their family and community history and their future roles as adult men and women. In western Africa, people also learned history by listening to the stories of griots. Griots were people who were specially trained to memorize and recite history.

African Folklore

Traditional beliefs and myths, many about birds, were passed down from generation to generation in ancient Africa through storytelling. Several birds, including hawks and eagles, were believed to be messengers of the gods. Many tales told of migrating birds bringing **fertility** with them. In others, birds were reincarnated, or reborn, humans. Taking eggs from a bird's nest was thought to bring bad luck.

Schools and Universities

The spread of Islam and Arabic writing through ancient Africa led to the founding of many schools and universities. One of the largest centers of learning was Timbuktu. Located in present-day Mali, it had prominent libraries, three universities, and 180 schools by the 1100s. Students were taught the Arabic language and script by Islamic scholars, and memorized the Qur'an, the Muslim holy book. They also learned Islamic history, mathematics, astronomy, and sciences.

*Mancala **is an African game still played today that archaeologists think dates back to 1500 B.C. Game pieces are moved from one position, or pit, on the game board to another. Ancient Africans thought mancala tested intelligence.***

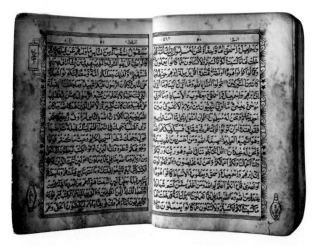

Muslims believe that the Qur'an contains the revelations of God to Muhammad, the Arab prophet and founder of Islam.

The Spreading of Education

Sonni Ali Ber, the first Songhai king, was famous for expanding the Mali empire of Songhai. His army captured the Mali city-state of Timbuktu, important as a trading post as well as a learning center. Sonni Ali Ber was not a popular ruler because he did not think education was important. After his death in 1492, the new king appointed scholars from Timbuktu to the government and made learning important to the Songhai people.

The Swahili Coast is a 1,500-mile (2,400-kilometer) stretch of coastline along present-day Kenya and Tanzania. It was a central area of trade between Africa and other countries, including Europe, Asia, and the Middle East, starting around 100 A.D. The Swahili Coast is named after the Swahili language spoken by the people in the region. Over time, this African language adopted many Arabic and Persian words and became the language of trade.

Ancient Mesoamerica

1400 B.C.–1521 A.D.

Ancient Mesoamerica was located where the countries of southern Mexico, Belize, Guatemala, Honduras, El Salvador, Nicaragua, Costa Rica, and Panama are today. Over thousands of years, the Olmec, Zapotec, Maya, and Aztec peoples invented their own languages and writing systems. The Maya and the Aztecs created writing systems of hieroglyphs, a number system, and a calendar that was very accurate.

Sign Language

Recording with hieroglyphic symbols began with the Olmec, and continued with the Zapotecs. Although they were fierce warriors, the Zapotecs also studied astronomy and developed the first writing system in the Americas. Using hieroglyphs, they recorded their history on stone tablets. It was the Maya, however, who first developed an entire language. The Maya used a familiar picture, or glyph, that symbolized an entire word. The Maya also invented an alphabet that helped them sound out a word when there was not a glyph to represent it. The Aztecs also used glyphs, but unlike the Maya, did not have an alphabet.

Translating

In the last 100 years, archaeologists have learned how to read some Maya glyphs by studying three surviving Maya manuscripts, called codices. Each codice is full of stories about which days are best for planting maize, hunting, or going into battle. The codices have allowed archaeologists to identify glyphs for a number of the Maya gods and understand some of their astronomical and mathematical calculations.

Book-making

Ancient Mesoamericans made folding-screen books with pages made from either deer skin or bark paper. These manuscripts were huge compared to the size of modern books. The Dresden Codex is a Maya book of astronomy that is 74 pages long and eleven feet (three meters) wide when laid out flat. The Maya used mostly bark paper for their books. To make the paper, they soaked the inner bark of trees in water to soften the wood. The bark was then beaten with stones, or a wooden mallet, until smooth. The soft, flat bark was whitewashed and painted by scribes, who were skilled in the art of writing and reading glyphs.

This stone pillar, or stele, in Quirigua, Guatemala, depicts ancient Maya glyphs.

An Aztec codex, or book, was sometimes painted on parchment made from tree bark. Aztec scribes recorded religious stories, their people's history, and even weather forecasts in books.

Creation Stories

The greatest stories told throughout Mesoamerica were those from a book called *Popol Vuh*. *Popol Vuh* begins with the story of creation, and includes legends of superhero ball-playing twins Hunahpn and Xbalanque. *Popul Vuh* was written in hieroglyphs by the Maya, but was destroyed by Spanish priests who burned all books after they landed in Mesoamerica in 1519. In 1558, a Mayan who had learned to write using Latin letters recorded the stories from *Popol Vuh* once again. The book was kept and forgotten in a church in Guatemala for over 100 years. It has since been found and translated into many languages.

Short Months

The Maya and Aztecs developed complex calendars to measure time. Each month had 20 days and there were two calendar years, one with 260 days and one with 365 days. The two calendars coincided every 52 years. This point in time was important to the ancient Mesoamericans. The Maya feared that the sky would fall or that the world might end if the gods were not satisfied. The Aztec marked the 52-year point with the New Fire Festival that lasted twelve days. During the festival there was fasting and human **sacrifice**.

Fortune-Telling Machines

The 260-day calendar moved in a repeating cycle. The calendar was used to predict the future, to name babies, and to choose lucky dates for battles and marriages, building houses, or sowing crops. Each day had its own god and good or bad fortune associated with it. The repeating cycle of 20 days has been compared to an endless fortune-telling machine.

The 365-day calendar had eighteen months of 20 days each. It was based on the solar cycle. For the Maya, there was an unlucky five-day period at the end of the calendar. For the Aztecs, these five "days of nothing" were festival days when people wore their best clothes and took part in dancing and singing. This was also the time when priests performed sacrifices.

The circular Aztec calendar was used by priests to remember religious festivals.

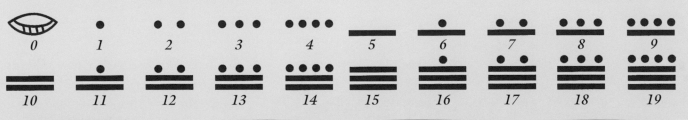

Mayan Math

In Mayan math, there were three symbols to represent numbers. A dot represented one, a bar meant five, and a symbol that looked like a sea shell stood for zero. The symbols were arranged vertically to make larger numbers and arranged from bottom to top. Merchants used the counting system when tallying sums during trade.

Math was also used to plan construction of buildings and in astronomy to help figure out dates and times.

A second system of writing numbers was also used. Instead of dots and bars, heads of gods were carved to represent the numbers from one through twelve. As numbers progressed from smallest to biggest, more facial features were added.

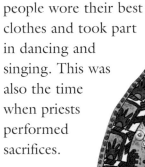

0	1	2	3	4	5	6	7	8	9
10	11	12	13	14	15	16	17	18	19

Ancient South America

900 B.C.–1572 A.D.

Hundreds of cultures lived in and around the Andes mountains, the most powerful being the ancient Inca civilization. Many ancient South American societies had their own languages but did not have writing systems. They used storytelling and other methods to record information instead. Important facts, such as taxes, were recorded on a string called a *quipu* using a system of knots.

Inca Languages

The Incas allowed conquered peoples to speak their own languages, but they also insisted that everyone learn and understand the Inca language, Quechua. This was the language used by the Inca government. Among themselves, people spoke their native language. There were over 700 languages spoken within the Inca empire. One of these, Aymara, is the official language of modern-day Bolivia. Quechua is still spoken by millions of people in South America today.

Learning

Children in ancient South America learned practical skills by helping adults with their work. Children helped plant and harvest crops in the fields, and they also helped women with household tasks, such as preparing meals. They learned about their culture by listening to stories and legends told by the elders. The Incas sent only children of nobles to school. Sons of noble Inca families went to school in Cuzco for four years to learn the Quechua language. They also took lessons in history, religion, astronomy, and mathematics. Daughters of noble families were sometimes chosen to work in the temples, where they were taught to weave textiles and make objects from gold, such as ceremonial masks.

Becoming an Adult

Children of Andean societies became adults and could marry as soon as they reached puberty. Inca boys from noble families had to take lessons on Inca tradition and morals. They were tested to prove their intelligence and courage. If they passed the test, they were given a weapon, such as a spear, and decorative earplugs to show that they had become men.

Ancient South Americans, such as the Chimú, often depicted details about the way their gods looked and what they did on textiles.

Quipus

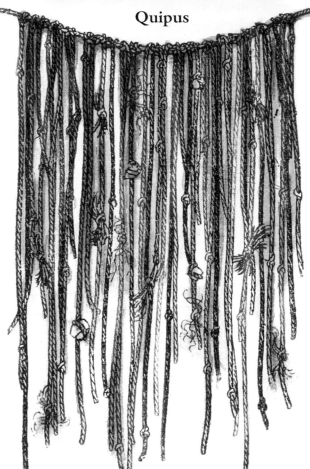

Quipus

Quipus

The Incas recorded information by using a *quipu*, a long string with shorter, colored strings tied to it. Each color represented something, such as corn, and the different types of knots represented numbers. A *quipucayamoc* was an expert in making and decoding *quipus*. It took four years of study to become a *quipucayamoc*. Administrators in each Inca province used the *quipu* system to record the number of births and deaths in the province, as well as the amount of woven cloth sent to Cuzco as tax. *Quipu* was also used to keep track of the size of llama herds and the amount of grain that farmers grew. The *quipus* were carried to Cuzco by trained runners called *chasquis*. Although historians know what kind of information was recorded on *quipus*, they do not know how to decode them.

The quipu *was a complicated method of record-keeping. Each string represented a piece of information, such as how many babies were born that year.*

Mountain Runners

Inca administrators could not communicate with each other easily because the empire was so large, and there were no vehicles or horses to travel the length of the empire. Trained runners, called *chasquis*, were used to deliver messages between government administrators. *Chasquis* were stationed in small stone huts that stood every four miles (6.5 km) or so on the Inca road network called the Royal Road, which criss-crossed the length of the Inca empire covering over 14,000 miles (22, 500 km). These huts, called *tambos*, had food and water supplies for the *chasquis*. When a *chasqui* received a message, he ran as fast as he could to the next *tambo* and gave the message to the *chasqui* there. Messages could be carried about 150 miles (240 km) a day like this.

Chasquis *were also used to deliver special goods, such as fresh fish, to the Sapa Inca.*

Ancient Rome

Rome's ideal location and climate made it attractive to waves of settlers. Each new group influenced the next through the religion, language, or culture it left behind. An ancient group, or tribe, of nomadic **hunters** called the Latins introduced their language to Romans. Latin later became the language of Rome. Education was important to Romans because it trained children to obey orders. Obedient children were thought to be more loyal to Rome and Roman beliefs.

753 B.C.–476 A.D.

Language and Writing

Two thousand years ago, the ancient Roman rulers spread Latin throughout their empire. When the Roman empire fell in the fifth century, Italy split into many different kingdoms. The language spoken by the people changed over the following centuries. However, Latin continued to be used in churches, courts, and universities as a language of religion and learning. Latin slang developed into modern languages such as Italian, French, and Spanish.

Education System

In early Rome, parents taught their children at home. Children were taught by their mothers until they were about seven years old. They learned math, reading, and writing. After age seven, girls were taught how to run a household and boys learned their father's trade, were given tutors, or went to a local school. At school, boys memorized tables of measurement, including length, liquid measure, area, and money. Pupils copied the writings of Latin authors onto wax writing tablets using a sharpened stick called a stylus.

Roman boys work on their writing.

Higher Education

At age twelve, some boys went on to higher education. Sons of **patricians** who wanted a position in government needed to learn how to deal with people and influence their opinions. Some boys studied military strategy, so they could be officers in the Roman army. At fifteen, boys officially became men and put on the **toga** of manhood. A young man was then sent to study with his father's patrician friends before entering the military at age seventeen.

Calendars and Mathematics

In 46 B.C., Emperor Gaius Julius Caesar improved the twelve-month Roman calendar. This calendar, called the Julian calendar, was based on the studies of Egyptian astronomers. The month of July was renamed in Julius Caesar's honor, since it was the month he was born. March was named after Mars, the god of war. August was named after Emperor Caesar Augustus.

Making Laws

In the early days of the **republic**, Rome's rules, or laws, were published on bronze plates called the twelve tablets. The tablets contained laws on land ownership, inheritance, trespassing, contracts and eventually criminal laws and the punishments for crimes.

Philosophy and Writing

Romans adopted ways of learning, called philosophies, from Greece and other empires they conquered or traded with. Roman men, young and old, studied different philosophies in schools. Sometimes, Rome's emperors thought the philosophies were dangerous because they made people question the emperor's power or decisions he made. Rome had many writers and poets who were philosophers. Seneca was a writer and philosopher who wrote about maintaining order and the rule of wise people. His views got him into trouble with emperor Claudius, who banished him from the senate. The poet Virgil wrote a massive twelve volume poem called the *Aeneid*. The *Aeneid* was a history of the first settlers of Rome. The writer Ovid wrote books about the gods, and Horace wrote long poems called satires which made fun of Roman society. The works of many famous Roman authors and poets survived and are still studied today.

Roman arithmetic was difficult because numbers were represented by letters. For calculations requiring multiplication and division, they likely used pebbles in a row, like an abacus.

Cicero was an orator, or great speaker, who made many famous speeches in the Roman senate.

Is Latin a Dead Language?

The Roman alphabet is the basis for the alphabet used by many modern languages. The letters J, U, and W were added after the fall of the empire. The other 23 letters were the same as the upper case letters in the alphabet today. Many words in modern English are closely related to Latin words. For example: *Vendo* means "I sell" in English. A person who sells things is a vendor. *Video* means "I see" in English. A video is a movie on tape. *Liber* means "book" in English. Books are borrowed from the library.

Ancient Japan

Japan is made up of a chain of volcanic islands in the Pacific Ocean, 120 miles (200 km) from the east coast of China. The ancient Japanese borrowed a system of writing from China and altered it to suit their own language. Over time, three different styles of writing developed in Japan.

300 B.C.–1582 A.D.

Chinese Influence

People in ancient Japan traded with people from ancient Persia, India, China, and Korea. As trade between the nations grew, the Japanese began to borrow some of the traditions of these other cultures. The Japanese adopted Chinese styles of writing, artwork, and government until 894 A.D. After that, the people of ancient Japan changed the Chinese customs to fit with their own ideas and way of life.

"Hospitality" written in **hiragana.**

Murasaki Shikibu, author of one of Japan's most famous books, the Genji Monogatari.

The abacus was a counting instrument that school children used for solving math problems.

Writing

Japanese words are written according to sounds rather than letters. For example, two or three English letters might be combined to create one Japanese sound. This sound is expressed as one symbol, or character. Three types of writing systems were used in ancient Japan. The first was called *kanji*. In *kanji*, Japanese words were written using Chinese characters. Around 800 A.D., a script based on the way Japanese syllables sounded, called *hiragana*, developed. *Hiragana* was a simplified version of *kanji*. The Japanese called it "women's hand" since mostly women used it at first. *Katakana* was a script first used by Buddhist monks, students, and men. It was based on Japanese syllables, so the writer did not need to know Chinese to use the script.

Going to School

Only the privileged went to school in ancient Japan. Children from noble families were taught to read and write. They also studied math, history, poetry, and government. Children were taught by **Confucian** scholars and by Buddhist priests. Peasant children did not go to school, but they learned their parents' work by helping them.

Buddhism

The religion of Buddhism began in India in 528 B.C. Buddhism is based on the teachings of Siddhartha Gautama, known as the Buddha or "Enlightened One." The Buddha believed that the only way for people to avoid suffering was for them to stop wanting things. The Buddha taught that people could achieve a peaceful state of mind through **meditation**. Buddhism eventually spread through Asia and China and was brought to Japan by a visiting Buddhist monk in 552 A.D. Later, rulers sent students, scholars, and monks to China to study Buddhism. Buddhists built temples for worship throughout the countryside. Over time, followers of **Shinto** adopted some Buddhist beliefs.

Literature

The *Kojiki*, or the *Record of Ancient Matters*, was the first Japanese book written in 712 A.D. A book of myths and history, it described many ways of divination, or telling the future. Fortune-telling was important to the ancient Japanese, who believed that there were good and bad times for certain actions, such as going to war. The most common method of divination was to write a question, such as what the next season's weather or outcome of crops would be like, on a turtle shell or a cow's shoulder blade bone. Then the bone was heated until it cracked. A diviner studied the shape of the crack, then interpreted it as either a positive or negative answer to the question.

Between 794 and 1195, most of Japan's great writers were women. One of Japan's most famous books is the *Genji Monogatari*, meaning *Tale of Genji*, written around 1120 A.D. by Murasaki Shikibu. She lived in the emperor's court and wrote stories about the power struggles between the noble ladies who lived there. Genji, the hero of the story, is the emperor's son and goes through many struggles to find love.

Written Law

Japan's Taiho Code of 701 A.D. and Yoro Code of 718 A.D. stated how crimes should be punished, and how the government should be run. The laws were designed to make people obedient to the emperor. People who did not pay their debts were sold into slavery, as were thieves. People who committed violent crimes were executed.

Poetry

Traditional Japanese poetry is based on patterns of syllables. It does not have to rhyme. Early Japanese poems, called *tanka*, always had 31 syllables and were meant to make the reader feel one emotion. Today, the most famous style of Japanese poetry is *haiku*, which is a three-line poem with 17 syllables. The first collection of Japanese poetry was the *Manyoshu*, or *Collection of Myriad Leaves* (below). Some of these poems express the Japanese love for nature, and sadness for all beautiful things, because they must die eventually.

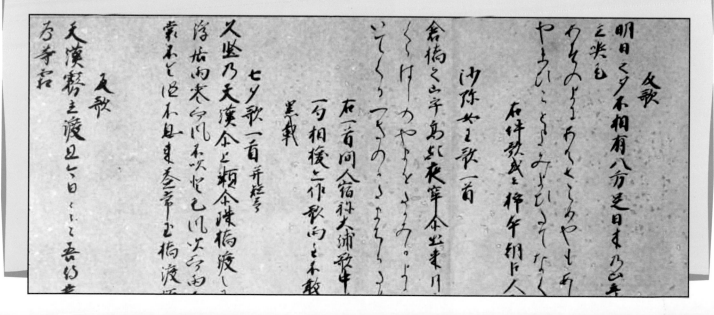

Ancient Celts

The Celts were the dominant civilization in Europe from 600 B.C. to 50 B.C. Known throughout the ancient world for their music, stories, and intricate artwork, the Celts did not actually write down their history. Instead, they passed on information through stories. Clan members, usually druids, memorized the stories and re-told them to others.

800 B.C.–43 A.D.

Who Were the Celts?

There were at least fifteen different Celtic groups. Historians refer to them together as the Celts because they shared the same original language and way of life. An important early Celtic group was the La Tène culture, which arose around 475 B.C. in present-day Switzerland and France. From the La Tène culture, Celtic language and styles of artwork and metalwork emerged.

Spoken Languages

Celtic groups in different areas of Europe spoke slightly different forms of the Celtic language. The most common language spoken by the Celts that lived in present-day France was Gaulish. The Celts in Britain spoke British, which was nothing like modern English. The Celts in Ireland spoke a language known as Gaelic. Beginning around 100 B.C., Celts began to use Latin instead of their own language as the Romans slowly conquered their lands. By 400 A.D., most of the Celtic languages were no longer used. In some areas, the languages survived, such as Brittany in France, Wales and Scotland in Britain, and in Ireland.

Writing

At least 500 years after the Celts were introduced to the Greek alphabet, they developed their own alphabet for writing called the Ogham script. The Ogham alphabet was made up of 25 letters, with consonants written as a series of vertical or horizontal lines. Vowels were written as dots. Archaeologists have found many gravestones and stones used to mark boundaries engraved with Ogham script in Britain and Ireland.

According to Irish legend, Ogham script was invented by the god Ogma.

Wandering Bards

Musicians and poets, known as bards, were highly respected, as their job was to learn the Celtic histories, stories, and legends and recite them as songs or poetry in each community. Bards also carried news between clans. Kings and queens held feasts in their homes or outdoors to keep clan members loyal to them. Everyone in the community was invited to attend and eat as much as they wanted. During the feasts, bards told tales and songs were sung.

Druid Schools

Druids were ancient Celtic priests and priestesses who served as the spiritual leaders of Celtic communities. Druids not only memorized Celtic stories, histories, laws, and religious beliefs, they also predicted the future by observing signs, called omens, in nature.

Each Celtic community had one or more druid who educated the children of nobles. Between the ages of seven and fourteen, girls and boys were taught Celtic histories and religious beliefs by listening to the druids. The druids did not believe in writing down their knowledge and students had to memorize all their teachings. Lessons were often sung in songs and students had to sing the songs until they were known by heart. Some children were also taught to read and write Greek script for everyday use.

Calendar

Pieces of a large bronze tablet were discovered in the town of Coligny in southern France in 1897. Archaeologists believe they are the remains of a Celtic calendar created by druids around 100 A.D. If the calendar is authentic, it shows that the Celts had twelve months, each consisting of 29 or 30 days. This made the year 354 days long. Every third year, an extra month was added to keep pace with the movement of the Earth around the sun.

England

In 43 A.D., the Roman army quickly conquered the Celtic groups of southeast England. Most Celts in England took on the Roman way of life, languages, and religion. The Romans never managed to conquer the Celts in the highlands of Scotland or in Ireland. In Ireland, Celtic laws, languages, and oral histories continued to survive.

Bards told their stories or poems accompanied by drum beats or simple music played on a flute or a stringed harp.

Myths and Legends

The Celts told stories of heroes and adventure. The stories were written down long after the Celtic culture declined, but they reveal the types of stories druids and bards told 2,000 years ago. One of the most famous stories is that of the Celtic hero, Cú Chulainn, from Ireland. In it, the queen of Ireland sends her men to capture a bull from Cú Chulainn's clan. Cú Chulainn single-handedly defends his people and protects the bull from the queen's men.

A mural of Cú Chulainn was painted in Belfast, Ireland.

29

Ancient Vikings

787 A.D.–1100 A.D.

The Vikings, also known as Norsemen, lived in the northern European countries of Norway, Sweden, and Denmark. Historians believe that their name may have come from the Norse word "vikingr," meaning pirate, or from "vik," meaning bay or harbor. The Vikings called their language donsk tunga, which means "the Danish tongue." Today, it is known as Old Norse. Vikings of the Scandinavian countries spoke this language, but with slightly different dialects. Vikings wrote their language by carving into bone, wood, or stone.

Writing

The Vikings' alphabet consisted of runes. The rune letters were made up of straight lines, which made carving them easier. Runes were used to engrave owners' names on belongings, and makers' names on goods they produced. Viking warriors decorated their swords and spears with runic characters. Receipts for goods were carved onto sticks, as were notes that were sent by messenger. The most famous examples of Viking writing are on rune stones. The Vikings engraved and set up large stones as memorials to famous Vikings or loved ones.

A Viking's Notebook

Historians believe that many Vikings could read and write runes. Children were also taught to read and write. Writing was practiced using a wooden tablet covered with melted wax. The wax was allowed to cool before being engraved with an iron knife or chisel to form the letters. Viking writing tablets were 12 inches (30 centimeters) long with a raised wooden border.

Stories and Poetry

Vikings were talented storytellers and poets. Their tales are of heroic warriors, brave sailors, and battles between gods and giants. None of these stories were written down on runes. Instead, they were spoken and passed down from generation to generation for hundreds of years. With Christianity came the Roman alphabet and the method of writing with ink on parchment. Around 1100 A.D., Icelandic poets and storytellers began to write down the stories and poems in the Icelandic language. Iceland's literature is the main written source of Viking stories.

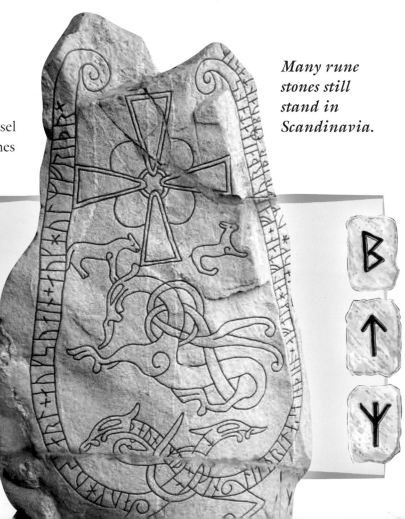

Many rune stones still stand in Scandinavia.

Reading Runes

There were not enough runes to represent all of the sounds in the Old Norse language. This meant that a single rune could represent several sounds, making runic inscriptions difficult to translate. The first line of a rune was usually written from left to right, the second from right to left, and so on. Some rune stones had lines of writing that ran up and down.

Sagas and Storytellers

One of the most famous books in Icelandic literature is the *Prose Edda*, written by Snorri Sturluson around 1200 A.D. The book contains mythological stories of the Norse, or Viking gods, goddesses, giants, and dwarves. Icelanders also wrote family histories and sagas. *Heimskringla*, also written by Snorri Sturluson, is a history of Norway and the famous warriors who lived there. Histories of heroic chieftains and tales of Norse gods and giants were spoken in verse to music and had riddles for the listeners to solve. Viking kings hired professional storytellers, called skalds, to make up poems about their bravery and skill in battle to recite at the royal court.

A Child's Life

Viking children began working when they were around five years old. Girls helped their mothers with weaving, cooking, and brewing beer and **mead**. The strongest girls were sometimes taught how to use weapons, such as knives, swords, and spears. Boys accompanied their parents as they worked on the farm to learn how to care for crops and animals. They were also taught how to fight with weapons, to navigate, and to build and repair ships. Some boys were sent to work as apprentices to blacksmiths or other artisans.

Place Names

Place names of many European countries reflect their Viking past. The Viking territory of Normandy, France, retains its name, which means "Land of the Northmen." In England, many towns have names ending in "by" or "thorpe," which are Viking words for towns and villages. These towns were built on the sites founded by Viking invaders. Greenland has also kept the name given to it by Erik the Red.

Russia's Name

When a Viking named Rurik settled in Eastern Europe, the local people called him Rus, which is the Slavic word for Viking. As his territory grew, the whole area became known as Russia.

The front cover of the Prose Edda *shows a number of figures from Norse mythology.*

Viking Surnames

Each Viking child was given his or her father's name as a surname. If a Viking named Niels Larsen called his son Jens, Jens' surname would be Nielsen. The endings "sen" or "son" meant "son." The name Jens Neilson meant "Jens, son of Niel." A last name that ended in "datter" or "dotter" meant "daughter."

Glossary

Buddha An ancient religious leader from India

Buddhism A religion founded by Buddha

city-state An independent city, usually walled for defense, and the surrounding towns and villages that depend upon it for defense

Confucianism A system of ethics and philosophy based on the teachings of Chinese scholar Confucius

fertility The ability to produce life

hymns Religious songs of praise and glory

illiterate Unable to read or write

invader A person who enters by force as an enemy

Islam A religion that follows the teachings of the prophet Muhammad

mead An alcoholic drink made from honey

meditate The act of thinking quietly

monk A member of a male religious community who has taken vows, such as silence or poverty

nomadic Moving from place to place

oral Spoken or passed from person to person

patrician The upper class of Roman society, including priests, army officers, and government

priestess Female priest

republic A government in which power is held by the people, who choose their leaders

sacrifice An offering to a god or goddess

Sapa Inca A ruler in ancient South America who controlled all of the land in the empire

scribe A person who makes a living by copying or recording text

Shinto The first religion practiced in Japan, which combined a love of nature with the worship of ancestor spirits

stylus A sharp, pointed instrument used for writing

toga A huge cloth that Romans draped in folds around the body

whitewashed Whitened with a mix of water and lime

Index

Websites

www.bbc.co.uk/history/ancient/
    Amazing images from historic sites around the world help give readers an in-depth look into many ancient cultures.

www.historyforkids.org/
    This site provides information on the history, food, clothing, technology, stories, and religion of many ancient cultures.

www.pbs.org/wgbh/nova/ancient/
    Interactive videos take readers through ancient civilizations.

www.archaeolink.com/ancient_trade_routes.htm
    Learn about the trade routes between ancient civilizations.

www.archaeolink.com/amazing_worlds_of_archaeology1.htm
    This site provides links to sites with archaeological information.

Further Reading

True Books: Ancient Civilizations series, Children's Press 2010

Biography from Ancient Civilizations: Legends, Folklore, and Stories of Ancient Worlds series, Mitchell Lane Publishers 2009

Ancient and Medieval People series, Benchmark books 2009

Ancient Civilizations series, Compass Point (Capstone) 2007